budgetbooks

FOLK SONGS

ISBN 978-1-4234-6764-9

HAL•LEONARD®
CORPORATION
7777 W. BLUEMOUND RD. P.O. BOX 13819 MILWAUKEE, WI 53213

In Australia contact:
Hal Leonard Australia Pty. Ltd.
4 Lentara Court
Cheltenham, Victoria, 3192 Australia
Email: ausadmin@halleonard.com.au

Visit Hal Leonard Online at
www.halleonard.com

CONTENTS

ACH DU LIEBER AUGUSTIN
(O My Dearest Augustine)

Eighteenth Century German Folk Song

Ach, du lie - ber Au - gus - tin,
Oh, my dear friend Au - gus - tine,

Au - gus - tin, Au - gus - tin. Ach, du lie - ber
Au - gus - tine, Au - gus - tine, oh, my dear friend

ALL MY TRIALS

African-American Spiritual

1. If re-li-gion was a thing that mon-ey could buy, _____ the rich would live _____ and the poor would die. _____
2. Go to sleep, my lit-tle ba-by, and don't you cry, _____ your dad was born _____ just to live and die. _____
3. Oh, I have a lit-tle book that sets me free, _____ my Bi-ble, _____ it spells "Li-ber-ty". _____
4. Yes, a man was born to suf-fer ag-o-ny, _____ his will to live _____ spells "Vic-to-ry". _____

All _____ my tri-als, Lord, _____ will

ALL THROUGH THE NIGHT

Welsh Folk Song

A-TISKET A-TASKET

Traditional

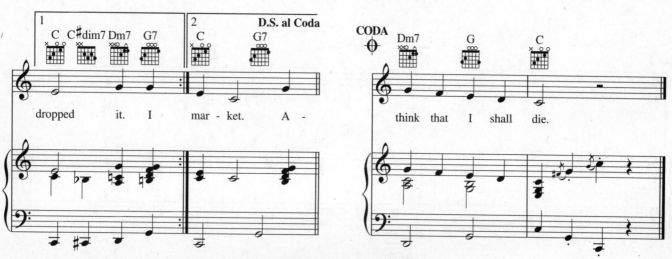

ALOHA OE

Words and Music by
QUEEN LILIUOKALANI

AMAZING GRACE

Words by JOHN NEWTON
from A Collection of Sacred Ballads
From Carrell and Clayton's *Virginia Harmony*
Traditional American Melody
Arranged by Edwino Excell

ALOUETTE

Traditional

Je te plu - me - rai la têt': Je te plu - me - rai la têt':

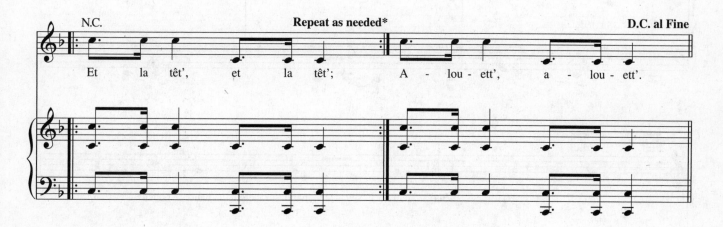

N.C.   **Repeat as needed***   **D.C. al Fine**

Et la têt', et la têt'; A - lou - ett', a - lou - ett'.

*Each chorus adds a new part of the body, in reverse order. For example, Chorus 3 is sung:

> Et le nez, et le nez;
> Et le bec, et le bec;
> Et la têt', et le têt';
> Alouett', Alouett'.
> Oh, *etc.*

2. le bec (*beak*)   6. les ailes (*wings*)
3. le nez (*nose*)   7. le dos (*back*)
4. les yeux (*eyes*)   8. les pattes (*feet*)
5. le cou (*neck*)   9. la queue (*tail*)

THE BANANA BOAT SONG
(Day Oh)

Jamaican Work Song

Freely

N.C.

Solo: Day oh. Day __ oh. Day da light, __ and I wan-na go home. __

Moderate Calypso

Six hand, sev-en hand, eight hand, bunch!

Day da light, ___ and I wan-na go home. ___

ARKANSAS TRAVELER

Southern American Folk Song

Hoe-down

AULD LANG SYNE

Words by ROBERT BURNS
Traditional Scottish Melody

Should auld ac-quain-tance

be for-got, and ___ nev - er brought to mind? Should

THE BEAR WENT OVER THE MOUNTAIN

Traditional

Moderately

Oh, the bear went o - ver the

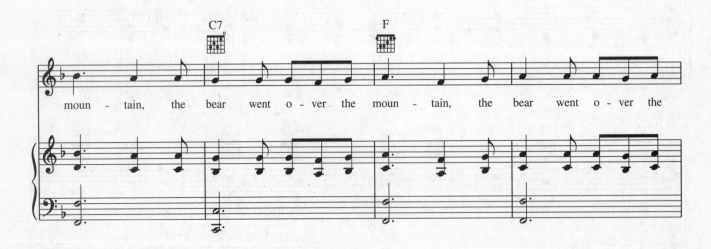

moun - tain, the bear went o - ver the moun - tain, the bear went o - ver the

moun - tain to see what he could see.

{ To see what he could
{ He saw what the oth - er

BEAUTIFUL BROWN EYES

Traditional

Oh, how I love you, my dar - ling. I
Life is so full ___ of trou - bles.

love you with all my heart. To -
Life is full of my woes.

BEAUTIFUL DREAMER

Words and Music by
STEPHEN C. FOSTER

Beau - ti - ful dream - - er,
Beau - ti - ful dream - - er,

wake un - to me;
out in the sea

star - light and dew - drops are wait - ing for
mer - maids are chant - ing the wild ___ lore -

thee. ___
lei. ___

Sounds of the rude world
O - ver the stream ___ let

BELIEVE ME, IF ALL THOSE ENDEARING YOUNG CHARMS

Words and Music by
THOMAS MOORE

BLACK IS THE COLOR OF MY TRUE LOVE'S HAIR

Southern Appalachian Folk Song

BLOOD ON THE SADDLE

Traditional

There was blood on the
cow - boy
pit - y the

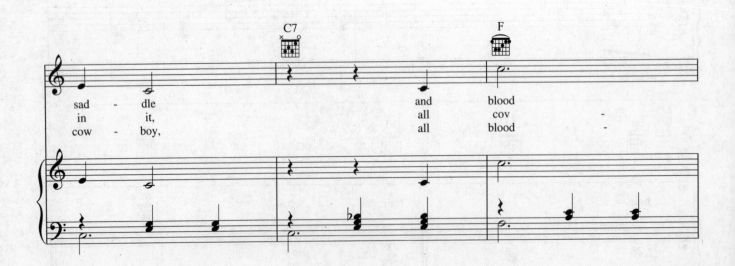

sad - dle and blood
in it, all blood cov -
cow - boy, all blood -

THE BLUE BELLS OF SCOTLAND

Words and Music attributed to
MRS. JORDON

Where, where, tell me where, does your _ high - land lad - die

dwell? Oh, where, tell me where, does your _

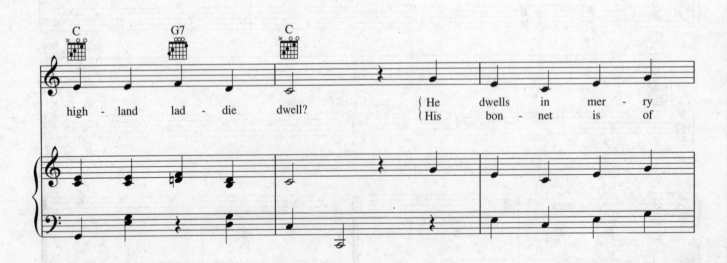

high - land lad - die dwell? He dwells in mer - ry
His bon - net is of

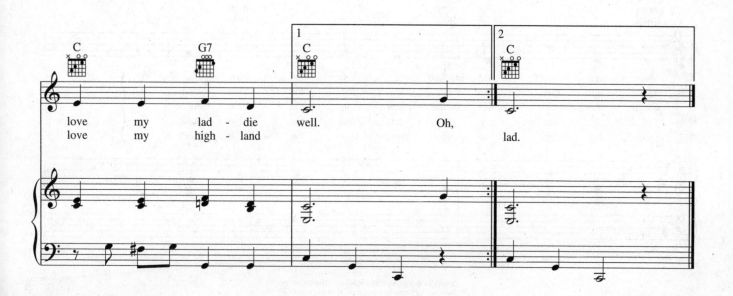

THE BLUE TAIL FLY
(Jimmy Crack Corn)

Words and Music by
DANIEL DECATUR EMMETT

BUFFALO GALS
(Won't You Come Out Tonight?)

Words and Music by
COOL WHITE (JOHN HODGES)

BURY ME NOT ON THE LONE PRAIRIE

Words based on the poem "The Ocean Burial"
by REV. EDWIN H. CHAPIN
Music by OSSIAN N. DODGE

CAMPTOWN RACES

Words and Music by
STEPHEN C. FOSTER

THE CAMPBELLS ARE COMING

Scottish Folk Song

CARELESS LOVE

Anonymous

CARNIVAL OF VENICE

By JULIUS BENEDICT

CHIAPANECAS

Traditional

CARRY ME BACK TO OLD VIRGINNY

Words and Music by
JAMES A. BLAND

CASEY JONES

Words by T. LAWRENCE SEIBERT
Music by EDDIE NEWTON

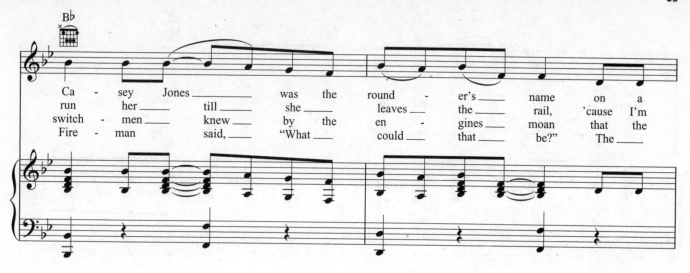

Ca - sey Jones _____ was the round - er's _____ name on a
run her _____ till _____ she the leaves _____ the _____ rail, moan 'cause I'm
Fire - man said, _____ "What _____ could en - gines that _____ be?" The _____

six - eight - wheel - er, boys, he won _____ his fame. The
eight hours late _____ with that west - ern mail. He
man at the throt - tle was _____ Ca - sey Jones. He
South - ern Pa - cif - ic and the San - ta Fe." Mis - sus

call - er called Ca - sey at a half _____ past four, _____
looked at his watch and his watch _____ was slow, _____ he
pulled up with - in two _____ miles of the place; _____
Jones sat on _____ her _____ bed _____ a - sigh - ing,

kissed his wife _____ at the sta - tion _____ door,
looked at the wa - ter and the wa - ter was _____ low. He
Num - ber _____ Four _____ stared him right in the _____ face.
just re - ceived a mes - sage that Ca - sey was dy - ing. Said,

mount - ed to the cab - in with his or - ders in his hand _____ and he
turned to the Fire - man said _____ "Boy, you'd bet - ter jump, _____ 'cause there's
Turned to the Fire - man said, _____ "Go to bed, chil - dren, and _____ hush _____ your _____ cry - ing 'cause you

took his fare - well trip _____ to that prom - ised land.
go - ing to reach Fris - co, but we'll all _____ be dead."
two Lo - co - mo - tives that's a - go - ing to bump."
got an - oth - er pa - pa on the Salt _____ Lake Line. Mis - sus

CIELITO LINDO
(My Pretty Darling)

By C. FERNANDEZ

Under my win - dow these swag - gers, _____
De - ba - jo de mi ven - ta - na _____

care - less of night and its dag - gers,_____ a char -
pa - sa las no - ches ron - dan - do_____ un cha -

ri - to,* reck - less fel - low,_____ with a
rri - to muy va - lien - te_____ que me es -

plain - tive voice and mel - low._____
tá a mi e - na - mo - ran - do._____

Char - ro** who stops at my grat - ing,_____
Ay cha - rri - to no me ron - des_____

* diminutive of Charro
** a rustic swain

COMIN' THROUGH THE RYE

By ROBERT BURNS

(Oh, My Darling)
CLEMENTINE

Words and Music by
PERCY MONTROSE

dar - ling, oh, my dar - ling Clem-en - tine, you are lost and gone for-

ev - er, dread-ful sor - ry, Clem-en - tine.

{ Walk - ing
{ She drove

tine.

Additional Lyrics

4. Ruby lips above the water,
   Blowing bubbles soft and fine,
   But alas, I was not swimmer,
   Neither was my Clementine.
   Chorus

5. Then the miner, forty-niner,
   Soon began to fret and pine,
   Thought he ought to join his daughter,
   So he's now with Clementine.
   Chorus

6. I'm so lonely, lost without her,
   Wish I'd had a fishing line,
   Which I might have cast about her,
   Might have saved my Clementine.
   Chorus

7. While I'm dreaming, I can see her,
   With a garment soaked in brine,
   Then she rises from the waters,
   And I kiss my Clementine.
   Chorus

THE CRAWDAD SONG

Traditional

With a lively beat, in 2

1. You get a line and I'll get a pole, my
2.-5. *(See additional lyrics)*

hon - ey. You get a line and

I'll get a pole, oh, babe.

Additional Lyrics

2. Get up old man, you slept too late, honey, (twice)
Get up old man, you slept too late,
Last piece of crawdad's on your plate,
Honey, sugar baby mine.

3. Get up old woman, you slept too late, honey, (twice)
Get up old woman, you slept too late, honey,
Crawdad man done passed your gate,
Honey, sugar baby mine.

4. What you gonna do when the lake goes dry, (twice)
What you gonna do when the lake goes dry,
Sit on the bank and watch the crawdads die,
Honey, sugar baby mine.

5. What you gonna do when the crawdads die, honey? (twice)
What you gonna do when the crawdads die,
Sit on the bank until I cry,
Honey, sugar baby mine.

DANNY BOY

Words by FREDERICK EDWARD WEATHERLY
Traditional Irish Folk Melody

DEEP RIVER

African-American Spiritual
Based on Joshua 3

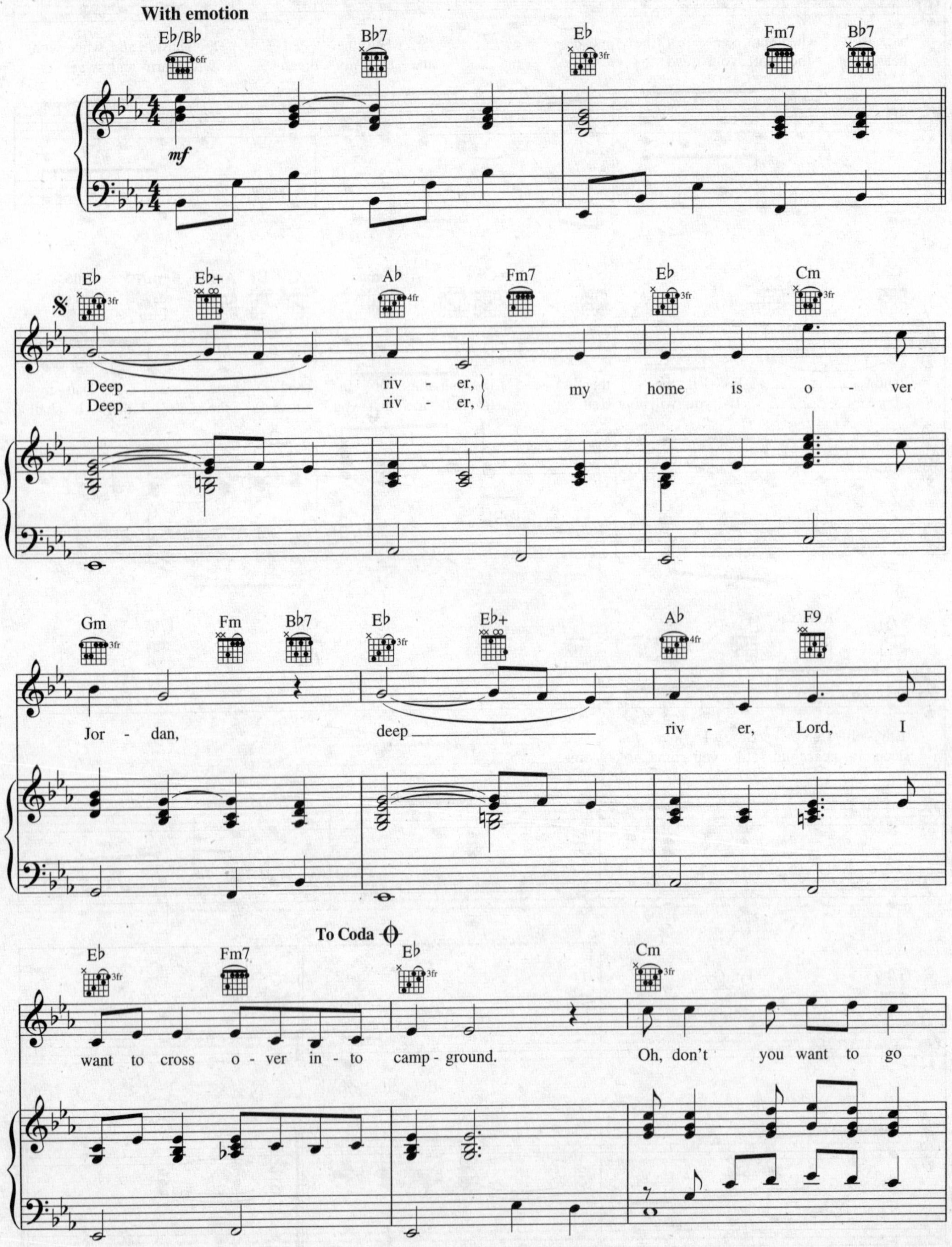

With emotion
Eb/Bb Bb7 Eb Fm7 Bb7
mf
Eb Eb+ Ab Fm7 Eb Cm
Deep river, my home is over
Deep river,
Gm Fm Bb7 Eb Eb+ Ab F9
Jordan, deep river, Lord, I
To Coda
Eb Fm7 Eb Cm
want to cross over into campground. Oh, don't you want to go

DOWN BY THE RIVERSIDE

African American Spiritual

DRINK TO ME ONLY WITH THINE EYES

Lyrics by BEN JONSON
Traditional Music

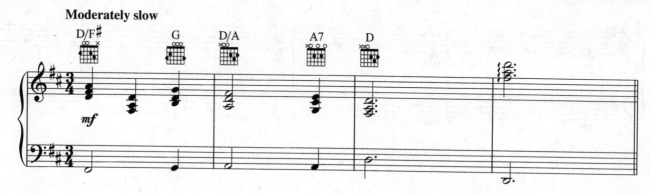

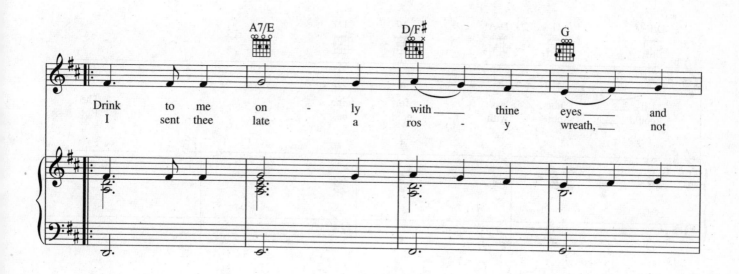

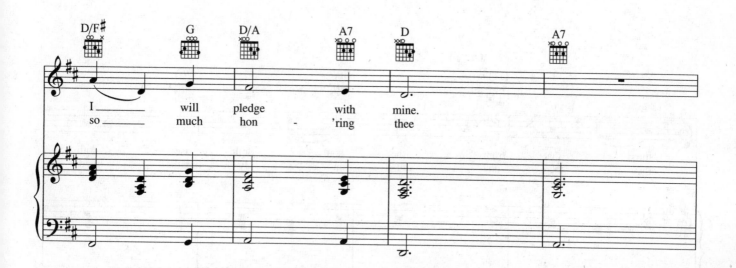

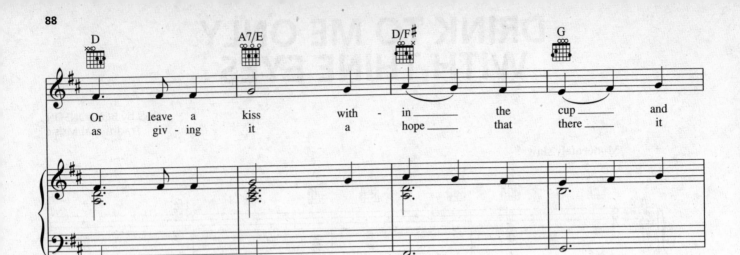

Or   leave a   kiss   with - in _____ the   cup _____ and
as   giv - ing   it   a   hope _____ that   there _____ it

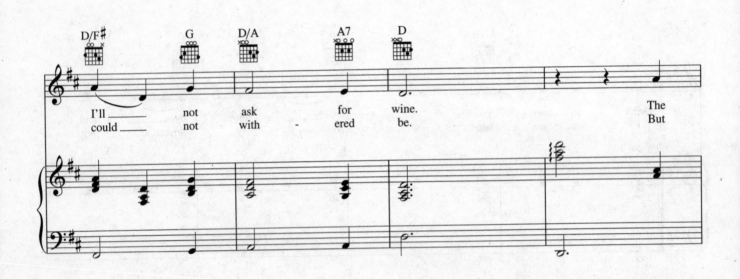

I'll _____ not   ask   for   wine.   The
could _____ not with - ered   be.   But

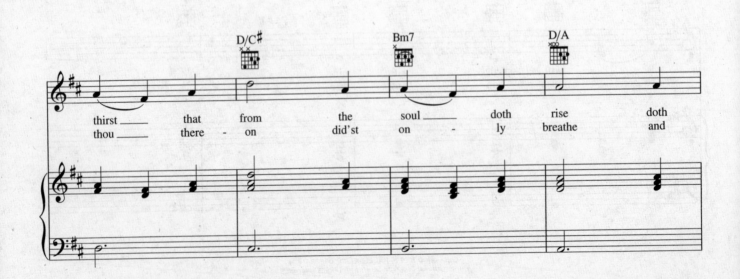

thirst _____ that from   the   soul _____ doth   rise   doth
thou _____ there - on   did'st   on - ly   breathe   and

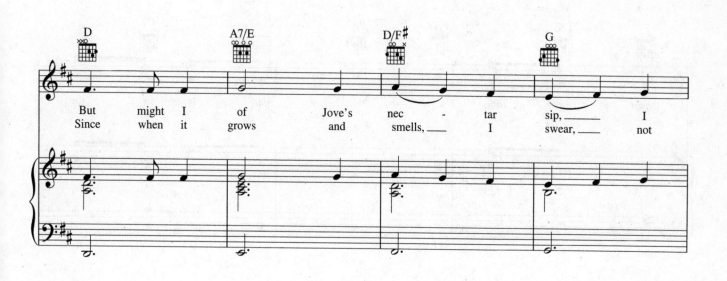

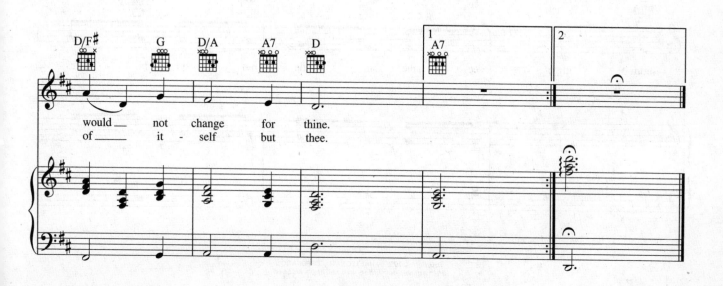

DOWN BY THE STATION

Traditional

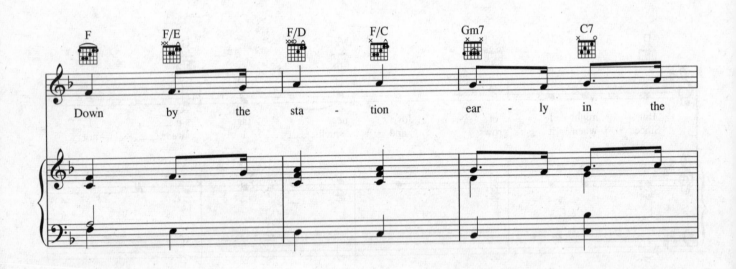

Down by the sta - tion ear - ly in the

morn - ing, see the lit - tle puf - fer - bil - lies

all in a row. See the en - gine

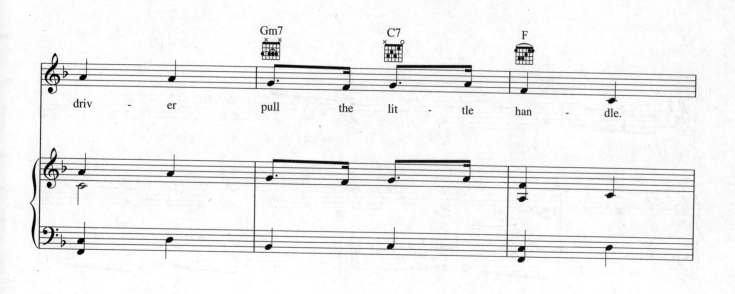

driv - er pull the lit - tle han - dle.

Choo! Choo! Toot! Toot! Off they go.

DOWN IN THE VALLEY

Traditional American Folk Song

1. Down in the val - ley, the
2.-4. *(See additional lyrics)*

val - ley so low, _____ hang your head o - ver,

hear the wind blow. _____ Hear the wind blow, love, oh

hear the wind blow, _____ hang your head o - ver,

hear the wind blow. _____

Additional Lyrics

2. Give my heart ease, love, oh give my heart ease,
   Think of me, darling, oh give my heart ease.
   Write me a letter and send it to me,
   Care of the jailhouse in Raleigh, N.C.

3. Write me a letter with just a few lines,
   Answer me, darling, and say you'll be mine.
   Roses love sunshine and violets love dew,
   Angels in Heaven know I love you!

4. This gloomy prison is far from you, dear,
   But not forever; I'm out in a year.
   I make this promise to get straight and true,
   And for a lifetime to love only you!

THE DRUNKEN SAILOR

American Sea Chantey

Additional Lyrics

Take him an' shake 'im, an' try an' wake 'im,
Earlye in the mornin'!

Give him a dose o' salt an' water,
Earlye in the mornin'!

Give him a taste o' the bosun's rope-end,
Earlye in the mornin'!

DRY BONES

Traditional

foot bone con-nect-ed to the leg bone, the leg bone con-nect-ed to the

knee bone, the knee bone con-nect-ed to the thigh bone, the

thigh bone con-nect-ed to the back bone, the back bone con-nect-ed to the

neck bone, the neck bone con-nect-ed to the head bone, oh,

DU, DU LIEGST MIR IM HERZEN
(You, You Weigh on My Heart)

German Folk Song

THE ERIE CANAL

Traditional New York Work Song

THE FOGGY, FOGGY DEW

Traditional

FOR HE'S A JOLLY GOOD FELLOW

Traditional

FRANKIE AND JOHNNY

Anonymous Blues Ballad

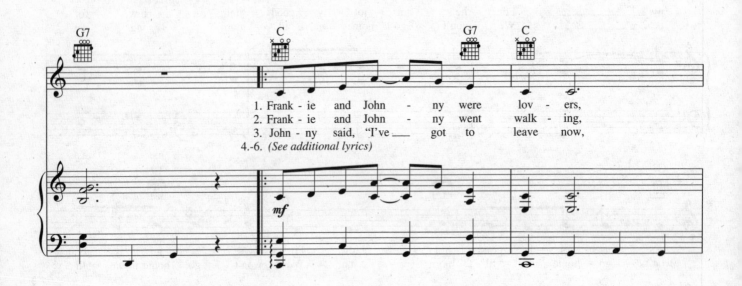

1. Frank-ie   and   John - ny   were   lov - ers,
2. Frank-ie   and   John - ny   went   walk - ing,
3. John - ny   said, "I've___ got   to   leave   now,
4.-6. *(See additional lyrics)*

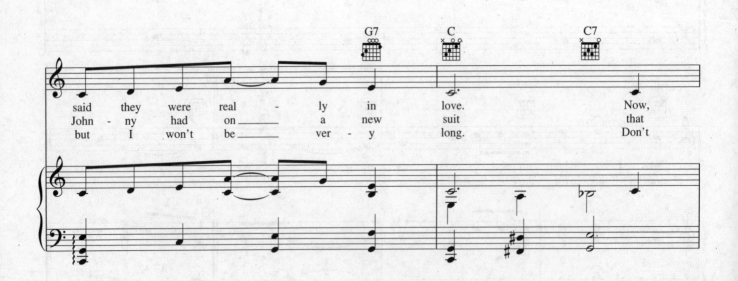

said   they   were   real - ly   in   love.   Now,
John - ny   had   on ___ a   new   suit   that
but   I   won't   be ___ ver - y   long.   Don't

Additional Lyrics

4. Frankie went down to the hotel,
   Looked in the window so high,
   There she saw her lovin' Johnny—
   Making love to Nellie Bly.
   Chorus

5. Johnny saw Frankie a-comin',
   Down the back stairs he did scoot,
   Frankie, she took out her pistol,
   Oh, that lady sure could shoot!
   Chorus

6. Frankie, she went to the big chair,
   Calm as a lady could be,
   Turning her eyes up, she whisper'd,
   "Lord, I'm coming up to Thee."
   Chorus

FREIGHT TRAIN

Words and Music by
ELIZABETH COTTEN

Freight train, freight train, run so fast.
When I'm dead, and in my grave,
When I die, and Lord, bur-y me deep

Freight train, freight train run so fast.
no more good times run here I crave.
way down on old Chest-nut Street.

FROG WENT A-COURTIN'

Please don't tell what train I'm on so they won't
Place the stones at my head and feet and tell 'em
Then I'll hear old Num - ber Nine __ as __

know what route I've gone.
that I've comes roll - in' by.
she

FROG WENT A-COURTIN'

Anonymous

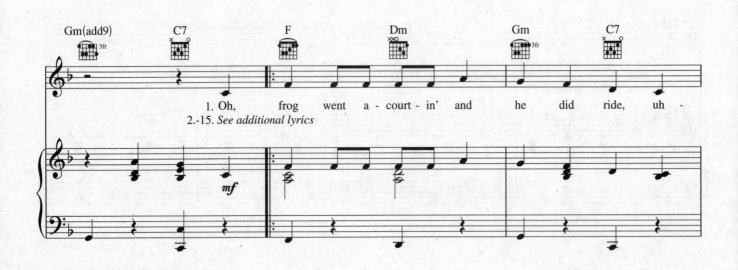

1. Oh, frog went a-court-in' and he did ride, uh-
2.-15. *See additional lyrics*

huh, uh-huh. Frog went a-court-in' and

he did ride, sword and pis - tol by his side, uh -

huh, uh - huh. (2.-15.) huh.

Additional Lyrics

2. Well, he rode down to Miss Mouse's door, uh-huh, uh-huh.
   Well, he rode down to Miss Mouse's door,
   Where he had often been before, uh-huh, uh-huh.

3. He took Miss Mousie on his knee, uh-huh, uh-huh.
   He took Miss Mousie on his knee,
   Said, "Miss Mousie, will you marry me?" Uh-huh, uh-huh.

4. "I'll have to ask my Uncle Rat, etc.
   See what he will say to that." etc.

5. "Without my Uncle Rat's consent,
   I would not marry the President."

6. Well, Uncle Rat laughed and shook his fat sides,
   To think his niece would be a bride.

7. Well, Uncle Rat rode off to town
   To buy his niece a wedding gown.

8. "Where will the wedding supper be?"
   "Way down yonder in a hollow tree."

9. "What will the wedding supper be?"
   "A fried mosquito and a roasted flea."

10. First to come in were two little ants,
    Fixing around to have a dance.

11. Next to come in was a bumble bee,
    Bouncing a fiddle on his knee.

12. Next to come in was a fat sassy lad,
    Thinks himself as big as his dad.

13. Thinks himself a man indeed,
    Because he chews the tobacco weed.

14. And next to come in was a big tomcat,
    He swallowed the frog and the mouse and the rat.

15. Next to come in was a big old snake,
    He chased the party into the lake.

FUNICULI, FUNICULA

Words and Music by
LUIGI DENZA

GIRL I LEFT BEHIND ME

Traditional Irish Folksong

GIVE ME THAT OLD TIME RELIGION

Traditional

Give me that old time re - li - gion, give me that old time re -

li - gion, give me that old time re - li - gion, it's good e - nough for

me. { It was good for the He - brew chil - dren, It was
{ It will do when the world's on fi - re, It will

GO TELL AUNT RHODY

Traditional

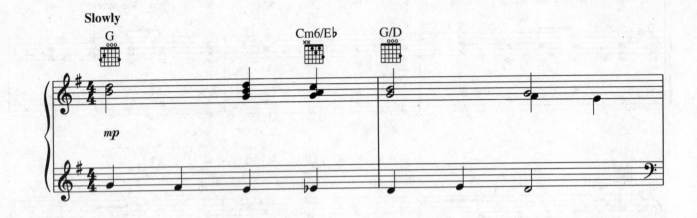

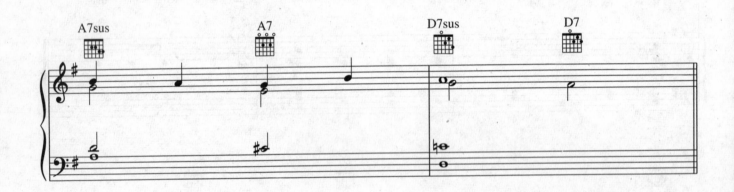

1. Go   tell   Aunt   Rho   dy,

2.-5. (See additional lyrics)

Additional Lyrics

2. The one she was saving, *(three times)*
   To make a feather bed.

4. The goslings are crying, *(three times)*
   Because their mama's dead.

3. The gander is weeping, *(three times)*
   Because his wife is dead.

5. She died in the water, *(three times)*
   With her heels above her head.

GO, TELL IT ON THE MOUNTAIN

African-American Spiritual
Verses by JOHN W. WORK, JR.

GOOBER PEAS

Words by P. PINDAR
Music by P. NUTT

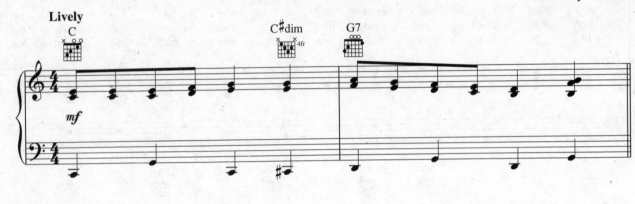

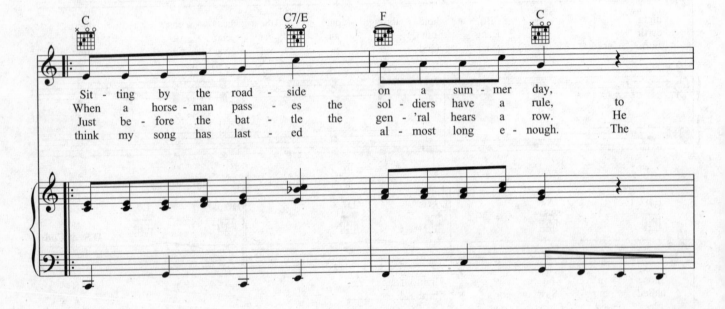

Sit - ting by the road - side on a sum - mer day,
When a horse - man pass - es the sol - diers have a rule, to
Just be - fore the bat - tle the gen - 'ral hears a row. He
think my song has last - ed al - most long e - nough. The

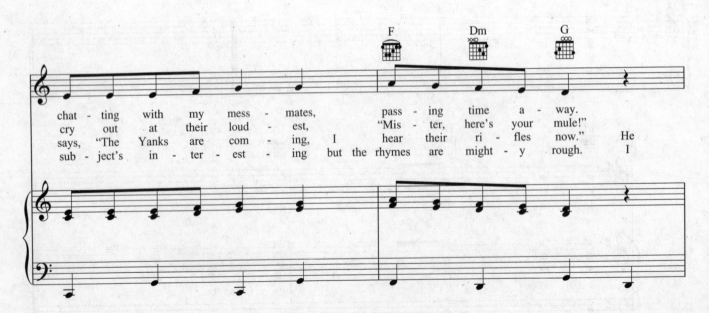

chat - ting with my mess - mates, pass - ing time a - way.
cry out at their loud - est, "Mis - ter, here's your mule!"
says, "The Yanks are com - ing, I hear their ri - fles now." He
sub - ject's in - ter - est - ing but the rhymes are might - y rough. I

GRANDFATHER'S CLOCK

By HENRY CLAY WORK

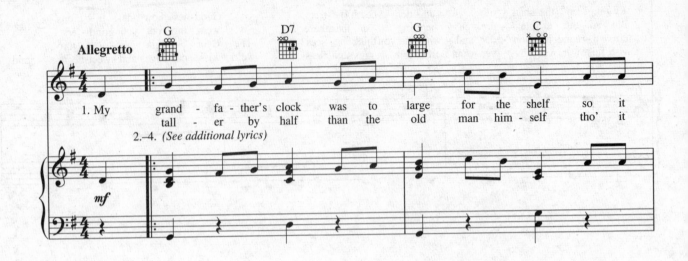

1. My grand-fa-ther's clock was to large for the shelf so it
tall-er by half than the old man him-self so tho' it
2.-4. *(See additional lyrics)*

stood nine-ty years on the floor. It was
weighed not a pen-ny-weight more. It was bought on the morn of the

Chorus

day that he was born and was al-ways his treas-ure and pride. But it stopped short

Additional Lyrics

2. In watching its pendulum swing to and fro,
Many hours had he spent while a boy;
And in childhood and manhood the clock seemed to know,
And to share both his grief and his joy.
For it struck twenty-four when he entered at the door,
With a blooming and beautiful bride.
Chorus

3. My grandfather said that of those he could hire,
Not a servant so faithful he found;
For it wasted no time, and had but one desire,
At the close of each week to be wound.
And it kept in its place, not a frown upon its face,
And its hands never hung by its side.
Chorus

4. It rang an alarm in the dead of the night,
An alarm that for years had been dumb;
And we knew that his spirit was pluming its flight,
That his hour of departure had come.
Still the clock kept the time, with a soft and muffled chime,
As we silently stood by his side.
Chorus

GREENSLEEVES

16th Century Traditional English

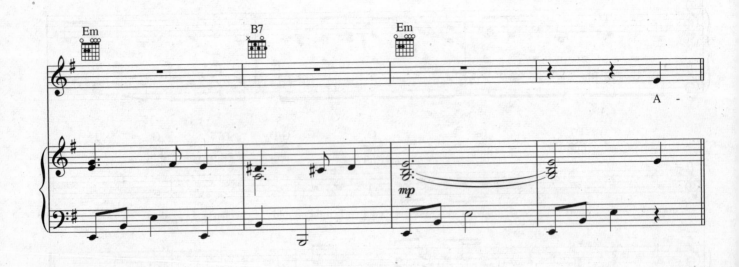

las,   my   love, _____ you   do   me   wrong _____ to
you   in - tend _____ thus   to   dis -   dain, _____ it
las,   my   love, _____ that   you   should   own _____ a
Green - sleeves,   now _____ fare - well,   a -   dieu; _____ to

GOOD NIGHT LADIES

Words by E.P. CHRISTY
Traditional Music

Good night, la-dies, good night, la-dies! Good night, la-dies, We're going to leave you now. Mer-ri-ly we roll a-long, roll a-long, roll a-long, mer-ri-ly we roll a-long, o'er the deep blue sea.

GUANTANAMERA

Cuban Folk Song

Additional Spanish Lyrics	Literal Translation	Additional English Lyrics
2. Mi verso es de un verde claro, Y de un carmin encendido, Mi verso es un ciervo herido, Que busca en el monte amparo. *Chorus*	2. My verses are soft green but also a flaming red. My verses are like wounded fauns Seeking refuge in the forest.	2. *I write my rhymes with no learning, And yet with truth they are burning, But is the world waiting for them? Or will they all just ignore them? Have I a poet's illusion, A dream to die in seclusion?* *Chorus*
3. Con los pobres de la tierra, Quiero yo mi suerte e char, El arroyo de la sierra, Me complace mas que el mar. *Chorus*	3. I want to share my fate With the world's humble. A little mountain stream pleases me More than the ocean.	3. *A little brook on a mountain, The cooling spray of a fountain Arouse in me an emotion, More than the vast boundless ocean, For there's a wealth beyond measure In little things that we treasure.* *Final chorus, in Spanish*

HE'S GOT THE WHOLE WORLD IN HIS HANDS

Traditional Spiritual

HAIL, HAIL, THE GANG'S ALL HERE

Words by D.A. ESROM
Music by THEODORE F. MORSE
and ARTHUR SULLIVAN

HAVA NAGILA
(Let's Be Happy)

Lyrics by MOSHE NATHANSON
Music by ABRAHAM Z. IDELSOHN

Ha - va na - gi - la ha - va na - gi - la

ha - va na - gi - la v' - nis - m' - cha

ha - va na - gi - la ha - va na - gi - la ha - va

HINKY DINKY PARLEY VOO

Author Unknown

HOME ON THE RANGE

Lyrics by DR. BREWSTER HIGLEY
Music by DAN KELLY

1. Oh, give me a home where the
2. of - ten at night when the
3.,4. *See additional lyrics*

buf - fa - lo roam, where the deer and the
heav - ens are bright, from the light of the

an - te - lope play, where
glit - ter - ing stars, have I

Additional Lyrics

3. Where the air is so pure and the zephyrs so free,
And the breezes so balmy and light;
Oh, I would not exchange my home on the range
For the glittering cities so bright.
Chorus

4. Oh, give me a land where the bright diamond sand
Flows leisurely down with the stream,
Where the graceful white swan glides slowly along,
Like a maid in a heavenly dream.
Chorus

THE HOUSE OF THE RISING SUN

Southern American Folk Song

Spend your lives ___ in sin and ___ mis - er - y ___ in the

house ___ of the Ris - ing Sun.

Well, ___ I've got one foot on the
is a house in

HOME SWEET HOME

Words by JOHN HOWARD PAYNE
Music by HENRY R. BISHOP

'Mid ___ pleas - ures and pal - a - ces though ___ we may
ex - ile from home, splen - dor daz - zles in
thee, I'll re - turn, o - ver - bur - dened with

roam, Be it ev - er so hum - ble, there's
vain, Oh, ___ give me my low - ly thatched
care, The ___ heart's dear - est sol - ace will

no ___ place like home; A charm ___ from the sky seems to
cot - tage a - gain; The birds ___ sing - ing gai - ly, that
smile ___ on me there. No more ___ from that cot - tage a

159

HUSH, LITTLE BABY

Carolina Folk Lullaby

I WISH I WERE SINGLE AGAIN

Words and Music by
J.C. BECKEL

I GAVE MY LOVE A CHERRY
(The Riddle Song)

Traditional

I'VE BEEN WORKING ON THE RAILROAD

American Folk Song

IF YOU'RE HAPPY
AND YOU KNOW IT

Words and Music by
L. SMITH

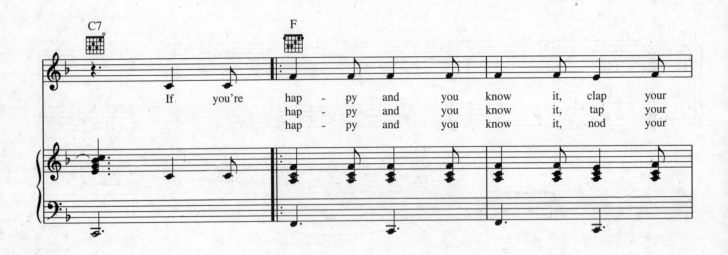

If you're hap - py and you know it, clap your
hap - py and you know it, tap your
hap - py and you know it, nod your

hands.   (clap,   clap)   If you're hap - py and you
toe.   (tap,   tap)   If you're hap - py and you
head.   (nod,   nod)   If you're hap - py and you

IN THE GOOD
OLD SUMMERTIME

Words by REN SHIELDS
Music by GEORGE EVANS

IN THE SHADE OF THE OLD APPLE TREE

Words by HARRY H. WILLIAMS
Music by EGBERT VAN ALSTYNE

THE IRISH WASHERWOMAN

Irish Folk Song

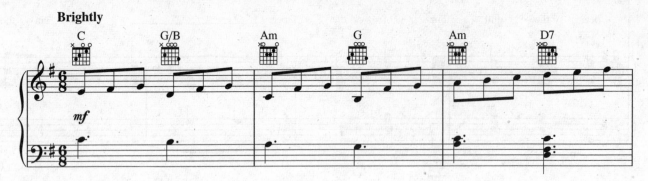

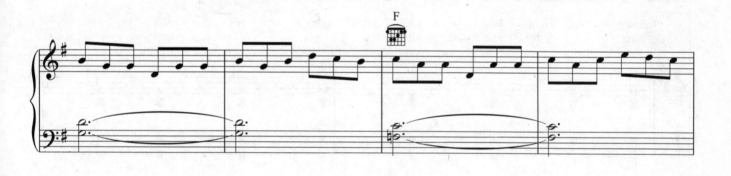

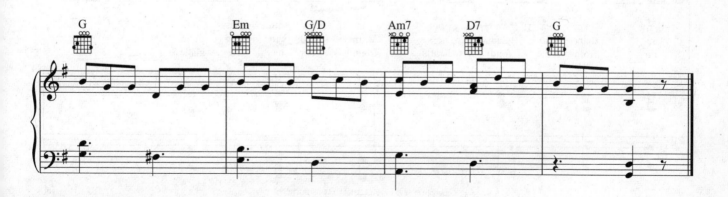

JEANIE WITH THE LIGHT BROWN HAIR

Words and Music by
STEPHEN C. FOSTER

dream of Jean-ie with the light brown hair,
long for Jean-ie with the day-dawn smile,
sigh for Jean-ie, but her light form strayed

borne like a va-por on the sum-mer air. I
ra-diant in glad-ness, warm with win-ning guile. I
far from the fond hearts 'round her na-tive glade. Her

JOHN BROWN'S BODY
(sung to the melody of "Battle Hymn of the Republic")

1. John Brown's body lies a-mouldering in the grave.
   John Brown's body lies a-mouldering in the grave.
   John Brown's body lies a-mouldering in the grave.
   His soul is marching on.

Chorus

   Glory, glory, hallelujah!
   Glory, glory, hallelujah!
   Glory, glory, hallelujah!
   His soul is marching on.

2. The stars of heaven are a-looking kindly down.
   The stars of heaven are a-looking kindly down.
   The stars of heaven are a-looking kindly down.
   On the grave of old John Brown.

Chorus

   Glory, glory, hallelujah!
   Glory, glory, hallelujah!
   Glory, glory, hallelujah!
   His soul is marching on.

3. He's gone to be a soldier in the army of the Lord.
   He's gone to be a soldier in the army of the Lord.
   He's gone to be a soldier in the army of the Lord.
   His soul is marching on.

Chorus

   Glory, glory, hallelujah!
   Glory, glory, hallelujah!
   Glory, glory, hallelujah!
   His soul is marching on.

4. John Brown's knapsack is a-strapped upon his back.
   John Brown's knapsack is a-strapped upon his back.
   John Brown's knapsack is a-strapped upon his back.
   His soul is marching on.

Chorus

   Glory, glory, hallelujah!
   Glory, glory, hallelujah!
   Glory, glory, hallelujah!
   His soul is marching on.

JOHN JACOB JINGLEHEIMER SCHMIDT

Traditional

LAVENDER'S BLUE

English Folk Song

JOHNNY, I HARDLY KNEW YOU

Traditional Irish Folk Song

Additional Lyrics

4. Where are your legs that used to run, hurroo, hurroo!
Where are your legs that used to run, hurroo, hurroo!
Where are your legs that used to run
When you went for to carry a gun?
Indeed your dancing days are done.
Johnny, I hardly knew ye.

5. I'm happy for to see you home, hurroo, hurroo!
I'm happy for to see you home, hurroo, hurroo!
I'm happy for to see you home
All from the island of Sulloon,
So low in flesh, so high in bone.
Johnny, I hardly knew ye.

6. Ye haven't an arm, ye haven't a leg, hurroo, hurroo!
Ye haven't an arm, ye haven't a leg, hurroo, hurroo!
Ye haven't an arm, ye haven't a leg,
Ye're an armless, boneless, chickenless egg.
Ye'll have to put with a bowl out to beg.
Johnny, I hardly knew ye.

JOSHUA
(Fit the Battle of Jericho)

African-American Spiritual

JUST A CLOSER WALK WITH THEE

Traditional
Arranged by KENNETH MORRIS

KUMBAYA

Congo Folk Song

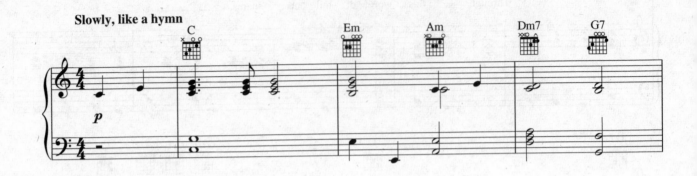

Kum - ba - ya, my Lord, _____ kum - ba -
cry - ing, Lord, _____ kum - ba -
pray - ing, Lord, _____ kum - ba -
need you, Lord, _____ kum - ba -

ya! _____ Kum - ba - ya, my Lord, _____ kum - ba -
ya! _____ Hear me cry - ing, Lord, _____ kum - ba -
ya! _____ Hear me pray - ing, Lord, _____ kum - ba -
ya! _____ Oh, I need you, Lord, _____ kum - ba -

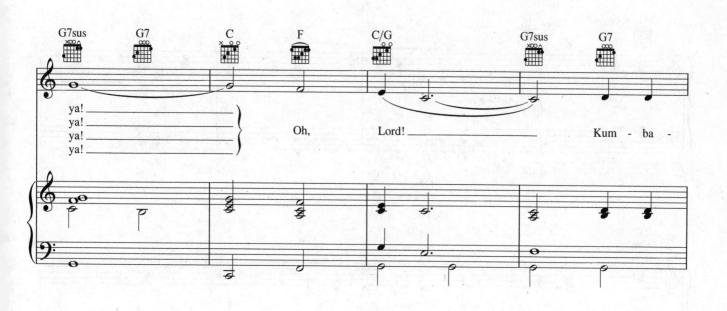

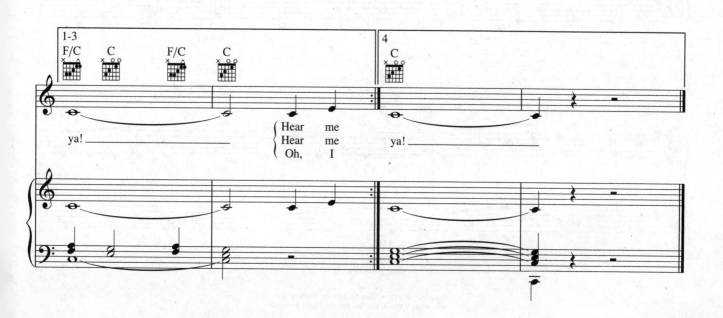

LA CUCARACHA

Mexican Revolutionary Folk Song

LI'L LIZA JANE
(Go Li'l Liza)

Words and Music by
COUNTESS ADA de LACHAU

1. I know a gal that I a - dore,
2. Down where she lives that the po - sies grow,
3. *(See additional lyrics)*

Li'l Li - za Jane.   'Way down south in
Li'l Li - za Jane.   Chick - ens 'round the

Bal - ti - more,   Li'l Li - za Jane.
kitch - en door,   Li'l Li - za Jane.

Additional Lyrics

3. I wouldn't care how far we roam, Li'l Liza Jane.
   Where she's at is home sweet home, Li'l Liza Jane.
   Oh, Eliza, Li'l Liza Jane!
   Oh, Eliza, Li'l Liza Jane.

LITTLE BROWN JUG

Words and Music by
JOSEPH E. WINNER

My wife and I, ___ we live a - lone ___ in a
you who make ___ my friends my foes, ___ 'tis

lit - tle log hut we call our own. ___ She loves gin ___ and
you who makes me wear old clothes. ___ Here you are ___ so

LOCH LOMOND

Scottish Folk Song

MAMA DON'T 'LOW

American Folk Song

1. Ma - ma don't 'low no danc - ing par - ties 'round
2. Ma - ma don't 'low no par - lor neck - in' 'round

3.-5. *(See additional lyrics)*

here, _____ oh no! My ma - ma don't 'low no
here, _____ oh no! My ma - ma don't 'low no

danc - ing par - ties 'round here. _____ Well,
par - lor neck - in' 'round here. _____ Well,

Additional Lyrics

3. Mama don't 'low no drums a-drummin' 'round here,
   Oh no! No banjos, guitars a-strummin' 'round here.
   Well, she's not here to rave and shout,
   And the Joneses living next door went out.
   Mama don't 'low no drums a-drummin' 'round here.

4. Mama don't 'low no loud mouth talkin' 'round here,
   Oh no! My mama don't 'low no loud mouth talkin' 'round here.
   Well, I don't care what mama don't 'low,
   Gonna shoot my mouth off anyhow.
   Mama don't 'low no loud mouth talkin' 'round here.

5. Mama don't 'low no nothin' going on here,
   Oh no! My mama don't 'low no nothin' going on here.
   Well, I don't see why my mama don't 'low,
   She was once as young as we are now.
   Mama don't 'low no nothin' going on here.

THE MAN ON THE FLYING TRAPEZE

Words by GEORGE LEYBOURNE
Music by ALFRED LEE

Left in the wide world to fret and to mourn, be -
e'er he ap - peared how the hall loud - ly rang with o -
fa - ther, he sighed, and her moth - er, she cried with to

trayed by a maid in her teens._____ Oh, the girl that I
va - tions from all peo - ple there._____ He'd smile from the
see her throw her - self a - way._____ 'Twas all no a -

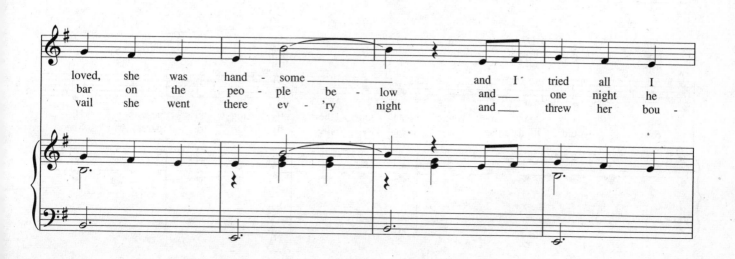

loved, she was hand - some _____ and I tried all I
bar on the peo - ple be - low and one night he
vail she went there ev - 'ry night and threw her bou -

move - ments were grace - ful, all girls he could please, and my love he
does all the work while he takes his ease, and that's what's be -

pur - loined a - way. Now, the
come of my Her
One love. _____
Some

Additional Lyrics

4. One night as usual I went to her dear home,
And found there her mother and father alone.
I asked for my love, and soon 'twas made known,
To my horror, that she'd run away.
She packed up her boxes and eloped in the night
With him, with the greatest of ease.
From two stories high he had lowered her down
To the ground on his flying trapeze.
Chorus

5. Some months after that I went into a hall;
To my surprise I found there on the wall
A bill in red letters which did my heart gall,
That she was appearing with him.
He'd taught her gymnastics and dressed her in tights
To help him live at ease.
He'd made her assume a masculine name,
And now she goes on the trapeze.
Chorus

MARIANNE

Traditional

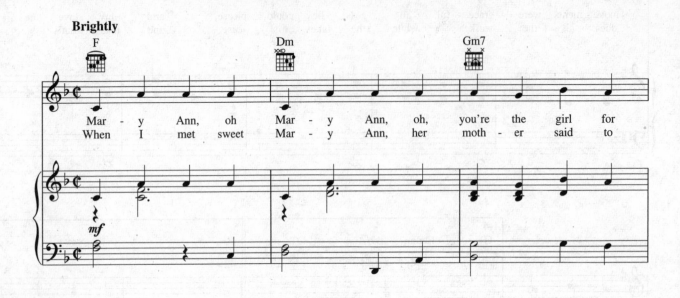

Mar - y Ann, oh Mar - y Ann, oh, you're the girl for
When I met sweet Mar - y Ann, her moth - er said to

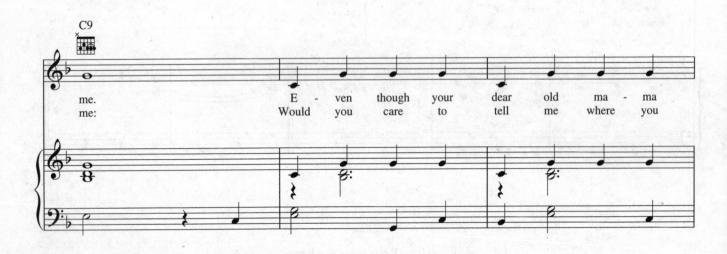

me.
me:
E - ven though your dear old ma - ma
Would you care to tell me where you

will not say, "Sí, sí."
stand fi - nan - cial - ly?
Mar - y Ann, oh,
She does not ap -

sea - side sift - in' sand, _____

all the lit - tle chil - dren love Mar - y Ann, _____

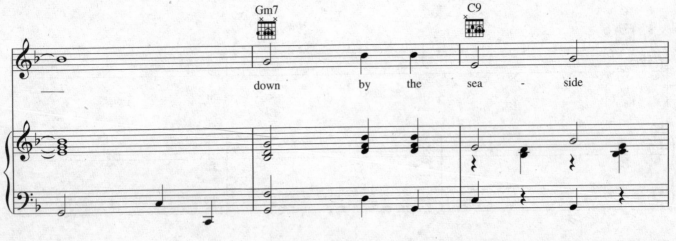

_____ down by the sea - side

sift - in' sand. _____

MY BONNIE LIES OVER THE OCEAN

Traditional

MICHAEL ROW THE BOAT ASHORE

Traditional Folk Song

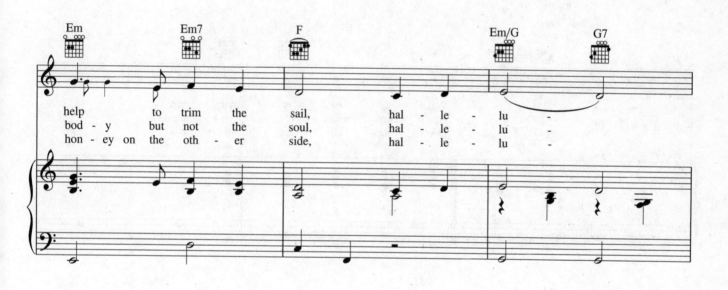

MIDNIGHT SPECIAL

Railroad Song

Wake up ev - 'ry morn - ing,
Don't know where it's go - ing,
Don't we all get ti - red

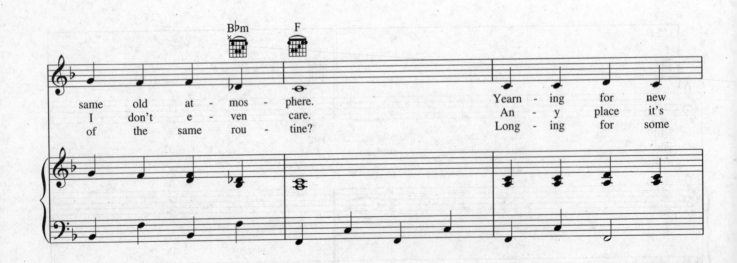

same old at - mos - phere.
I don't e - ven care.
of the same rou - tine?

Yearn - ing for new
An - y place it's
Long - ing for some

MOLLY MALONE
(Cockles & Mussels)

Irish Folk Song

221

MY OLD KENTUCKY HOME

Words and Music by
STEPHEN C. FOSTER

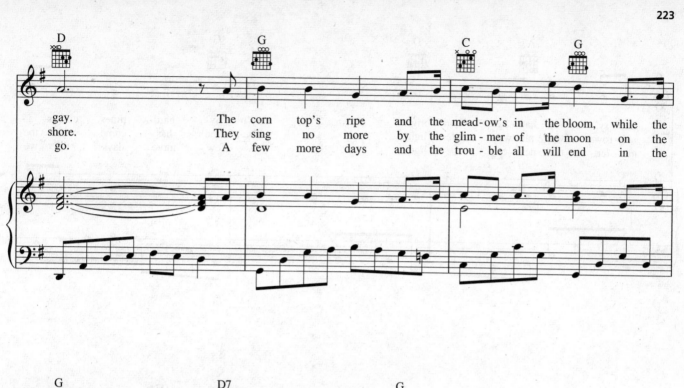

gay.
The corn top's ripe and the mead-ow's in the bloom, while the
shore.
They sing no more by the glim-mer of the moon on the
go.
A few more days and the trou-ble all will end in the

birds make mu - sic all the day.
The
bench by the old cab - in door.
The
field where the sug - ar canes___ grow.
A

young folks roll on the lit - tle cab - in floor,
all
day goes by like a shad - ow o'er the heart,
with
few more days for to tote the wea - ry load;
no

mer - ry,   all hap - py   and bright.   By'n by hard times comes a-
sor - row   where all was   de - light.   The time has come when the
mat - ter,   'twill nev - er   be light.   A few more days till we

knock - ing   at the door;   then   my   old   Ken - tuck - y   home,   good
old friends have   to part;   then   my   old   Ken - tuck - y   home,   good
tot - ter   on   the road;   then   my   old   Ken - tuck - y   home,   good

night!
night!   Weep   no more,   my   la - dy,   oh,
night!

weep no more to - day! We will sing one song for the

old Ken - tuck - y home, for the old Ken - tuck - y home far a - way.

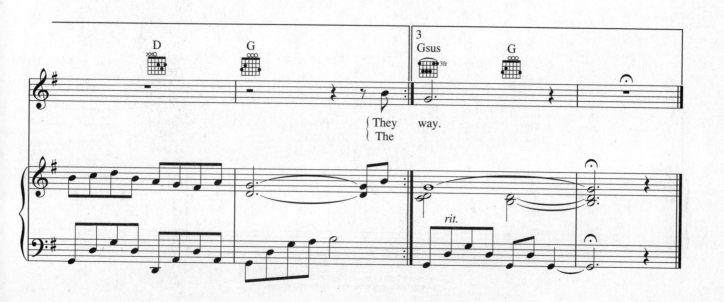

They way.
The

MY WILD IRISH ROSE

Words and Music by
CHAUNCEY OLCOTT

Lyrics:
My wild I-rish Rose, _____ the sweet-est flow'r that grows. _____

AUPRÈS DE MA BLONDE
(Nearby to My Dear One)

French Folk Song

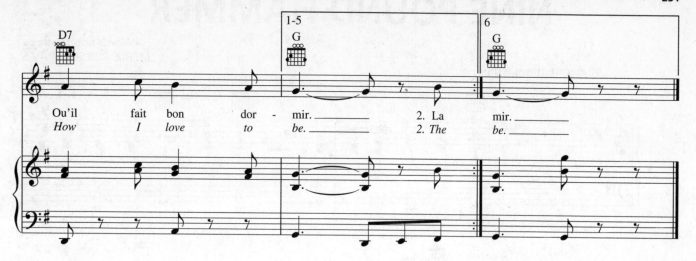

Ou'il fait bon dor - mir. _____ 2. La mir. _____
How I love to be. _____ 2. The be. _____

Additional Lyrics

2. La caill', la tourterelle,
   Et la jolie perdrix
   La caill', la tourterelle,
   Et la jolie perdrix,
   Et ma jolie colombe
   Qui chante jour et nuit.
   Refrain

3. Qui chante pour les filles
   Qui n'ont pas de mari,
   Qui chante pour les filles
   Qui n'ont pas de mari.
   Pour moir, ne chante guère,
   Car j'en ai un joli,
   Refrain

4. Dites-nous donc, la belle,
   Oú donc est vot' mari?
   Dites-nous donc, la belle,
   Où donc est vot' mari?
   Il est dans la Hollande,
   Les Hollandais l'ont pris,
   Refrain

5. Que donneriez-vous, belle,
   Pour avoir votre ami?
   Que donneriez-vous, belle,
   Pour avoir votre ami?
   Je donnerais Versailles,
   Paris et Saint-Denis,
   Refrain

6. Je donnerais Versailles,
   Paris et Saint-Denis,
   Je donnerais Versailles,
   Paris et Saint-Denis,
   Les tours de Notre-Dame,
   Et l'clocher d'mon pays;
   Refrain

2. *The quail, the grey woodpigeon,*
   And speckled partridge come,
   The quail, the grey woodpigeon,
   And speckled partridge come.
   My little dove, my dearest,
   That night and day doth croon.
   Refrain

3. *It's comforting the maidens*
   Unmarried and alone,
   It's comforting the maidens,
   Unmarried and alone.
   Sweet dove, don't sing for me then,
   A man, I have my own.
   Refrain

4. *O tell us, tell us, lady,*
   Where is your husband gone?
   O tell us, tell us, lady,
   Where is your husband gone?
   In Holland he's a prisoner,
   The Dutch have taken him.
   Refrain

5. *What would you give, my beauty,*
   To have your husband home?
   What would you give, my beauty,
   To have your husband home?
   Versailles I'd gladly give them
   And Paris and Notre Dame.
   Refrain

6. *Versailles I'd gladly give them,*
   And Paris and Notre Dame,
   Versailles I'd gladly give them,
   And Paris and Notre Dame,
   Saint Denis's Cathedral,
   And our church-spire at home.
   Refrain

NINE POUND HAMMER

Words and Music by
MERLE ROBERT TRAVIS

OH, THEM GOLDEN SLIPPERS

Words and Music by
JAMES A. BLAND

Oh, my gold-en slip-pers are ___ laid a-way, 'cause I
old ban-jo hangs ___ on the wall, 'cause it
good-bye chil-dren, I will have to go, where the

don't 'spect to wear 'em 'til my wed-ding day, and my long-tai'd coat that I
ain't been tuned since way last fall, but the folks all say we will
rain don't fall and the wind don't blow, and your ul-ster coats, why, you

NOBODY KNOWS THE TROUBLE I'VE SEEN

African-American Spiritual

OH! SUSANNA

Words and Music by
STEPHEN C. FOSTER

I come from Al - a-bam - a with my ban-jo on my knee, I'se
had a dream de ud-der night when eb-ry-ting was still; I

gwine to Lou -'si-an - a,   my true lub for   to see.   It
thought I saw Su-san-na dear a - com - ing down   de hill.   De

rained all night de day I left, de wed-der it   was dry,   the
buck - wheat cake was in her mouf, de tear was in   her eye;   I

OH WHERE, OH WHERE HAS MY LITTLE DOG GONE?

Words by SEP. WININER
Traditional Melody

Oh where, oh where has my lit-tle dog gone? Oh where, oh

where can he be? _____ With his ears cut short and his

tail cut long; oh where, oh where can he be? _____

OVER THE RIVER
AND THROUGH THE WOODS

Traditional

OLD BLACK JOE

Words and Music by
STEPHEN C. FOSTER

THE OLD CHISHOLM TRAIL

Texas Cowboy Song

ti yi u – pi u – pi yi.

2.,4.,5. I
3. It's

yi. Co – ma ti yi u – pi u – pi yi. _____

OLD FOLKS AT HOME
(Swanee River)

Words and Music by
STEPHEN C. FOSTER

far from de old folks at home.

THE OLD GRAY MARE

Words and Music by
J. WARNER

Oh! The old gray mare, she ain't what she used to be,

ain't what she used to be, ain't what she used to be. The

old gray mare, she ain't what she used to be, man-y long years a-

ON TOP OF OLD SMOKY

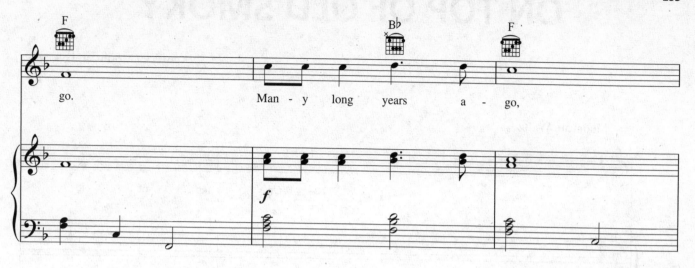

go. Man - y long years a - go,

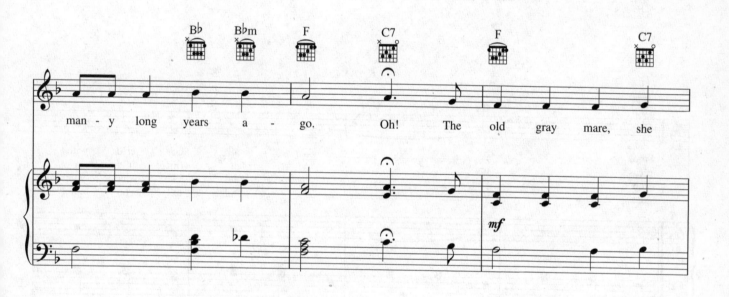

man - y long years a - go. Oh! The old gray mare, she

ain't what she used to be, man - y long years a - go.

ON TOP OF OLD SMOKY

Kentucky Mountain Folk Song

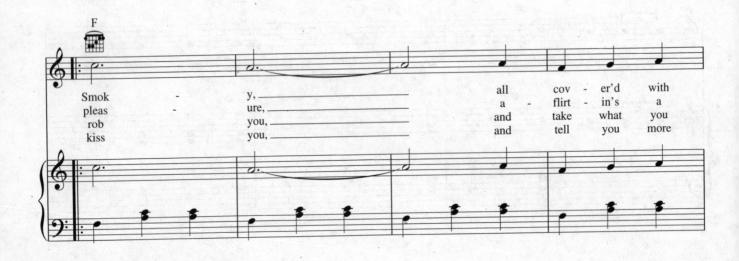

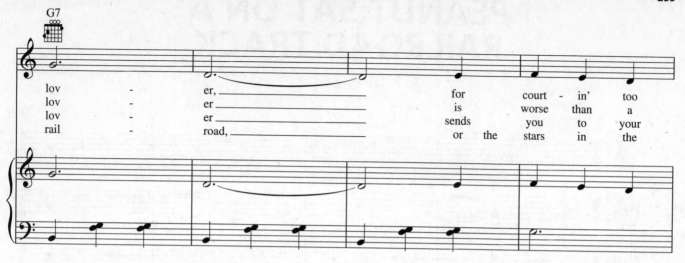

lov - er, _____ for court - in' too
lov - er _____ is worse than a
lov - er _____ sends you to your
rail - road, _____ or the stars in the

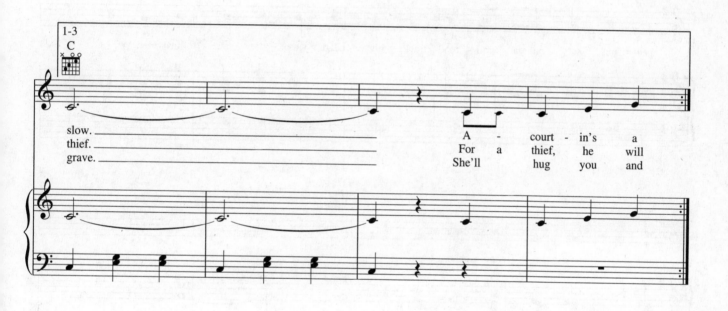

slow. _____ A - court - in's a
thief. _____ For a thief, he will
grave. _____ She'll hug you and

skies. _____

PEANUT SAT ON A RAILROAD TRACK

Traditional

RED RIVER VALLEY

Traditional American Cowboy Song

POLLY WOLLY DOODLE

Traditional American Minstrel Song

Additional Lyrics

4. Oh, I went to bed, but it wasn't no use,
   Singing polly-wolly-doodle all the day.
   My feet stuck out like a chicken roost,
   Singing polly-wolly-doodle all the day.
   Chorus

5. Behind the barn down on my knees,
   Singing polly-wolly-doodle all the day.
   I thought I heard a chicken sneeze,
   Singing polly-wolly-doodle all the day.
   Chorus

6. He sneezed so hard with the whooping cough,
   Singing polly-wolly-doodle all the day.
   He sneezed his head and tail right off,
   Singing polly-wolly-doodle all the day.
   Chorus

ROCK ISLAND LINE

Railroad Song

SAILORS HORNPIPE

Sea Chantey

ROCK-A-MY SOUL

African-American Spiritual

ROW, ROW, ROW YOUR BOAT

Traditional

A SUGGESTED ACTIVITY

"Row, Row, Row Your Boat" is a famous "round" that has been sung and enjoyed
by people of all ages. When sung correctly, the melody actually goes around and
around. Here's how it works: The singers are divided into two groups.
The first group sings the first line alone. At this point, the second group starts at
the beginning, while the first group continues with the second line. In this manner,
the groups are always exactly one line apart as the tune is repeated.
The last time through, the second group sings the final line alone just as the first group
sang the opening line alone. Try it. . . it's fun!

SAILING, SAILING

Words and Music by
GODFREY MARKS

Sail - ing, sail - ing

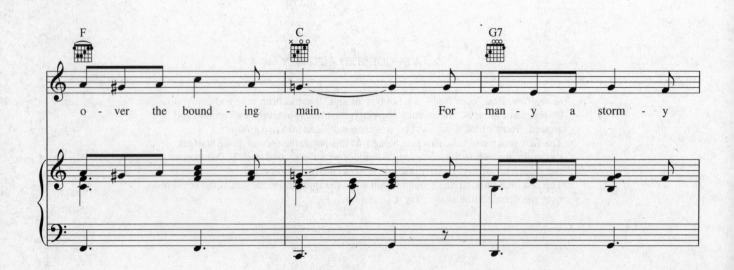

o - ver the bound - ing main. ____ For man - y a storm - y

SAINT JAMES INFIRMARY

Words and Music by
JOE PRIMROSE

SHE WORE A YELLOW RIBBON

Words and Music by
GEORGE A. NORTON

SANTA LUCIA

By TEODORO COTTRAU

SCARBOROUGH FAIR

Traditional English

1. Are you go - ing to Scar - bor - ough Fair?
2. Have {him / her} make me a cam - bric shirt,
3. Have {him / her} wash it in yon - der dry well,

4.-6. *(See additional lyrics)*

Pars - ley, sage, _____ rose - mar - y and
pars - ley, sage, _____ rose - mar - y and
pars - ley, sage, _____ rose - mar - y and

Additional Lyrics

4. Have him (her) find me an acre of land,
   Parsley, sage, rosemary and thyme.
   Between the sea and over the sand,
   And then he'll (she'll) be a true love of mine.

5. Plow the land with the horn of a lamb,
   Parsley, sage, rosemary and thyme.
   Then sow some seeds from north of the dam,
   And then he'll (she'll) be a true love of mine.

6. If he (she) tells me he (she) can't I'll reply:
   Parsley, sage, rosemary and thyme.
   Let me know that at least he (she) will try,
   And then he'll (she'll) be a true love of mine.

SCHOOL DAYS
(When We Were a Couple of Kids)

Words by WILL D. COBB
Music by GUS EDWARDS

282

SHE'LL BE COMIN' 'ROUND THE MOUNTAIN

Traditional

Additional Lyrics

3. Oh, we'll all go to meet her when she comes,
   Oh, we'll all go to meet her when she comes,
   Oh, we'll all go to meet her,
   Oh, we'll all go to meet her,
   Oh, we'll all go to meet her when she comes.

4. We'll be singin' "Hallelujah" when she comes,
   We'll be singin' "Hallelujah" when she comes,
   We'll be singin' "Halleluhah,"
   We'll be singin' "Hallelujah,"
   We'll be singin' "Hallelujah" when she comes.

SHENANDOAH

American Folk Song

1. Oh, Shen - an - doah, _____ I long to hear you, a -
2. Shen - an - doah, _____ I love your daught - er, a -
3. sev'n long years _____ since last I saw you, a -
4.-6. *(See additional lyrics)*

way, you roll - ing riv - er. _____
way, you roll - ing riv - er. _____ Oh, Shen - an - doah, _____ I love to
way, you roll - ing riv - er. _____ 'Tis sev'n long years _____ since last I

Additional Lyrics

4. Oh, Shenandoah, I love your daughter,
   Away, you rolling river.
   Oh Shenandoah, I'll come to claim her,
   Away, I'm bound away,
   'Cross the wide Missouri.

5. In all these years, whene'er I saw her,
   We have kept our love a secret.
   Oh! Shenandoah, I do adore her,
   Away, I'm bound away,
   'Cross the wide Missouri.

6. Oh, Shenandoah, she's bound to leave you,
   Away, you rolling river.
   Oh, Shenandoah, I'll not deceive you,
   Away, I'm bound away,
   'Cross the wide Missouri.

SHORT'NIN' BREAD

Plantation Song

SING A SONG OF SIXPENCE

Traditional

SOMETIMES I FEEL LIKE A MOTHERLESS CHILD

African-American Spiritual

SKIP TO MY LOU

Traditional

Lou, lou, skip to my lou, lou, lou, skip to my lou,

lou, lou, skip to my lou, skip to my lou, my dar - ling.

1. Lost my part - ner, what -'ll I do? Lost my part - ner, what -'ll I do?
2.-6. *(See additional lyrics)*

Additional Lyrics

2. I'll find another one, prettier than you.
   I'll find another one, prettier than you.
   I'll find another one, prettier than you.
   Skip to my lou, my darling.

3. Little red wagon, painted blue, etc.

4. Can't get a redbird, a bluebird'll do, etc.

5. Cows in the meadow, moo, moo, moo, etc.

6. Flies in the buttermilk, shoo, shoo, shoo, etc.

THE STREETS OF LAREDO

American Cowboy Song

Moderately

1. As

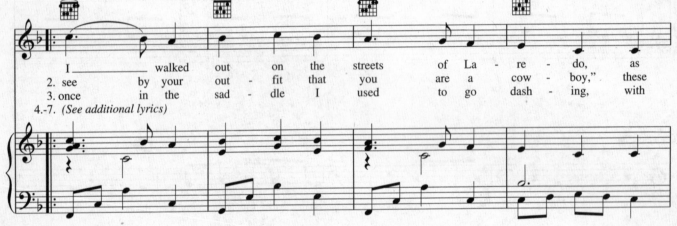

I _____ walked out on the streets of La - re - do, as
2. see by your out - fit that you are a cow - boy," these
3. once in the sad - dle I used to go dash - ing, with
4.-7. *(See additional lyrics)*

I _____ walked out in La - re - do one day, I
words he did say as I calm - ly went by. "Come
no one as say quick on the trig - ger as I. I

spied a young cow - boy all wrapped in white lin - en, all
sit down be - side me and hear my sad sto - ry, I'm
sat in a card game in back of the bar - room; got

wrapped in white lin - en and cold as the clay. "I dead.
shot in the breast, and I know I must die." "It was
shot in the back, and to - day I must die." "Get

Additional Lyrics

4. "Get six of my buddies to carry my coffin,
   And six pretty maidens to sing a sad song,
   Take me to the valley and lay the sod o'er me,
   For I'm a young cowboy who played the game wrong."

5. "Oh, beat the drum slowly and play the fife lowly,
   And play the dead march as they carry my pall.
   Put bunches of roses all over my coffin,
   The roses will deaden the clods as they fall."

6. "Go gather around you a crowd of young cowboys,
   And tell them the story of this my sad fate.
   Tell one and the other before they go farther,
   To stop their wild roving before it's too late."

7. "Go fetch me a cup, just a cup of cold water,
   To cool my parched lips," the cowboy then said.
   Before I returned, his brave spirit had left him,
   And gone to his Maker, the cowboy was dead.

SWEET BETSY FROM PIKE

American Folk Song

Moderately

1. Oh, don't you re-mem-ber sweet
2.-8. *(See additional lyrics)*

Bet-sy from Pike, who crossed the big moun-tains with her lov-er Ike; with

two yoke of cat-tle, a large yel-low dog, a ___ tall Shang-hai roos-ter, and

one spot-ted hog, say-ing good-bye, Pike Coun-ty, fare-well for a while. We'll

come back a-gain when we've panned out our pile. (2.-8.) panned out our pile.

Additional Lyrics

2. One evening quite early they camped on the Platte,
   'Twas near by the road on a green shady flat,
   Where Betsy, sore-footed, lay down to repose —
   With wonder Ike gazed on that Pike County rose.
   To Chorus

3. Their wagon broke down with a terrible crash,
   And out on the prairie rolled all kinds of trash,
   A few little baby clothes done up with care,
   'Twas rather suspicious, but all on the square.
   To Chorus

4. The Shanghai ran off, and their cattle all died;
   That morning the last piece of bacon was fried;
   Poor Ike was discouraged and Betsy got mad,
   The dog drooped his tail and looked wondrously sad.
   To Chorus

5. They soon reached the desert where Betsy gave out,
   And down in the sand she lay rolling about;
   While Ike, half distracted, looked on with surprise,
   Saying, "Betsy, get up, you'll get sand in your eyes."
   To Chorus

6. Sweet Betsy got up in a great deal of pain,
   Declared she'd go back to Pike County again;
   But Ike gave a sigh, and they fondly embraced,
   And they travelled along with his arm 'round her waist.
   To Chorus

7. They suddenly stopped on a very high hill,
   With wonder looked down upon old Placerville;
   Ike sighed when he said, and he cast his eyes down,
   "Sweet Betsy, my darling, we've got to Hangtown."
   To Chorus

8. Long Ike and sweet Betsy attended a dance;
   Ike wore a pair of his Pike County pants;
   Sweet Betsy was dressed up in ribbons and rings;
   Says Ike, "You're an angel, but where are your wings?"
   To Chorus

SWEET ROSIE O'GRADY

Words and Music by
MAUDE NUGENT

TAKE ME OUT TO THE BALL GAME

Words by JACK NORWORTH
Music by ALBERT VON TILZER

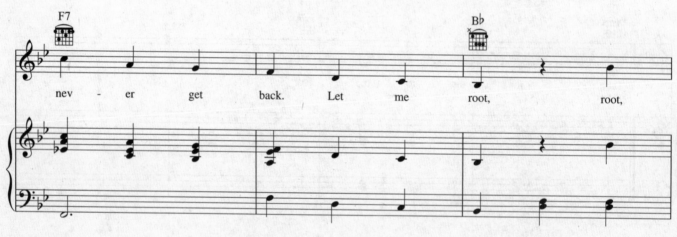

SWING LOW, SWEET CHARIOT

Traditional Spiritual

TARANTELLA

Traditional

THERE IS A TAVERN IN THE TOWN

Traditional Drinking Song

Moderately

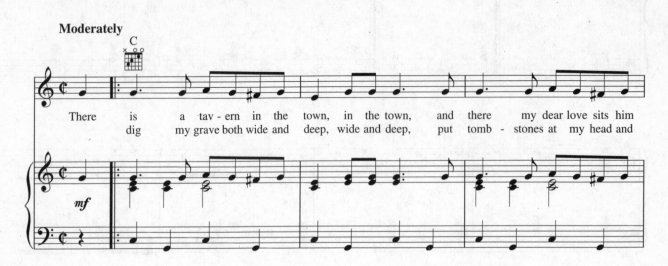

There is a tav-ern in the town, in the town, and there my dear love sits him
dig my grave both wide and deep, wide and deep, put tomb-stones at my head and

down, sits him down, and drinks his wine, 'mid laugh-ter free, and
feet, head and feet and on my breast, carve a tur-tle-dove, to

nev-er, nev-er thinks of me. }
sig-ni-fy I died for love. }
Fare thee well, for I must leave thee, do not

THERE'S A HOLE IN THE BUCKET

Traditional

Additional Lyrics

3. With what shall I fix it, dear Liza, etc.
4. With a straw, dear Henry, etc.
5. But the straw is too long, dear Liza, etc.
6. Then cut it, dear Henry, etc.
7. With what shall I cut it, dear Liza, etc.
8. With a knife, dear Henry, etc.
9. But the knife is too dull, dear Liza, etc.
10. Then sharpen it, dear Liza, etc.

11. With what shall I sharpen it, dear Liza, etc.
12. With a stone, dear Henry, etc.
13. But the stone is too dry, dear Liza, etc.
14. Then wet it, dear Henry, etc.
15. With what shall I wet it, dear Liza, etc.
16. With water, dear Henry, etc.
17. In what shall I carry it, dear Liza, etc.
18. In a bucket, dear Henry, etc.

19. There's a hole in the bucket, dear Liza, etc.

THIS OLD MAN

Traditional

With spirit

1. This old man, he played one, he played knick-knack on my drum.)
2. This old man, he played two, he played knick-knack on my shoe.) With a
3.-10. *(See additional lyrics)*

Chorus

knick-knack pad-dy-whack, give the dog a bone. This old man came roll-ing home. roll-ing home.

Additional Lyrics

3. This old man, he played three,
He played knick-knack on my knee.
Chorus

4. This old man, he played four,
He played knick-knack on my door.
Chorus

5. This old man, he played five,
He played knick-knack on my hive.
Chorus

6. This old man, he played six,
He played knick-knack on my sticks.
Chorus

7. This old man, he played seven,
He played knick-knack up to heaven.
Chorus

8. This old man, he played eight,
He played knick-knack at the gate.
Chorus

9. This old man, he played nine,
He played knick-knack on my line.
Chorus

10. This old man, he played ten,
He played knick-knack over again.
Chorus

THIS LITTLE LIGHT OF MINE

African-American Spiritual

TRAMP! TRAMP! TRAMP!

Words and Music by
GEORGE F. ROOT

THIS TRAIN

Traditional

Additional Lyrics

2. **This train don't carry no gamblers,** (*3 times*)
   No hypocrites, no midnight ramblers,
   This train is bound for glory, this train.

3. **This train don't carry no liars,** (*3 times*)
   No hypocrites and no high flyers,
   This train is bound for glory, this train.

4. **This train is built for speed now,** (*3 times*)
   Fastest train you ever did see,
   This train is bound for glory, this train.

5. **This train you don't pay no transportation,** (*3 times*)
   No Jim Crow and no discrimination,
   This train is bound for glory, this train.

6. **This train don't carry no rustlers,** (*3 times*)
   Sidestreet walkers, two-bit hustlers,
   This train is bound for glory, this train.

TURKEY IN THE STRAW

American Folksong

Chorus

Tur-key in the straw, *(whistle)* _____ tur-key in the hay,

(whistle) _____ roll 'em up and twist 'em up a high tuck-a-haw and __

hit 'em up a tune __ called __ Tur-key in the Straw. { Went __ } Tur-key in the Straw. { Met __ }

Additional Lyrics

4. Came to the river and I couldn't get across,
   Paid five dollars for an old blind hoss.
   Wouldn't go ahead, nor he wouldn't stand still,
   So he went up and down like an old saw mill.
   Chorus

5. As I came down the new cut road
   Met Mister Bullfrog, met Miss Toad.
   And every time Miss Toad would sing,
   Old Bullfrog cut a pigeon wing.
   Chorus

6. Oh, I jumped in the seat, and I gave a little yell,
   The horses run away, broke the wagon all to hell;
   Sugar in the gourd and honey in the horn,
   I never was so happy since the hour I was born.
   Chorus

TWINKLE, TWINKLE LITTLE STAR

Traditional

Twin - kle, twin - kle, lit - tle star,
When the blaz - ing sun is gone,

How I won - der what you are!
When he noth - ing shines up - on,

Up a - bove the world so high,
Then you show your lit - tle light,

Like a dia - mond in the sky. }
Twin - kle, twin - kle all the night. }

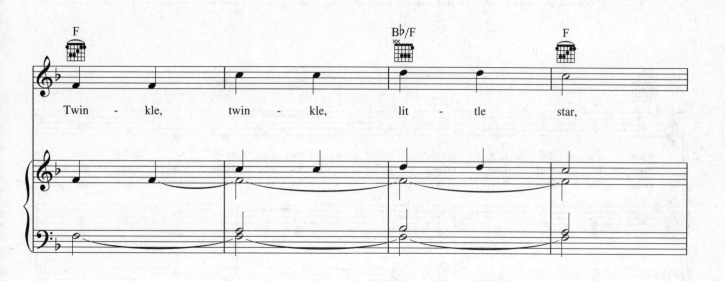

Twin - kle, twin - kle, lit - tle star,

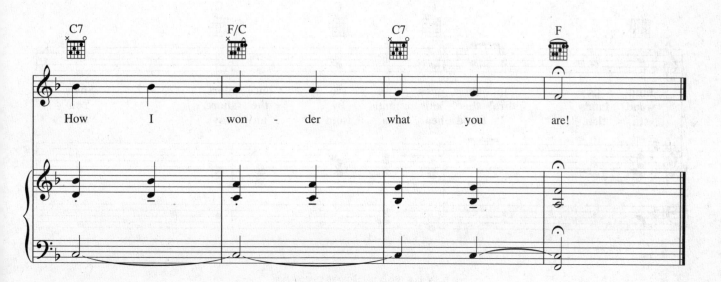

How I won - der what you are!

THE WABASH CANNON BALL

Hobo Song

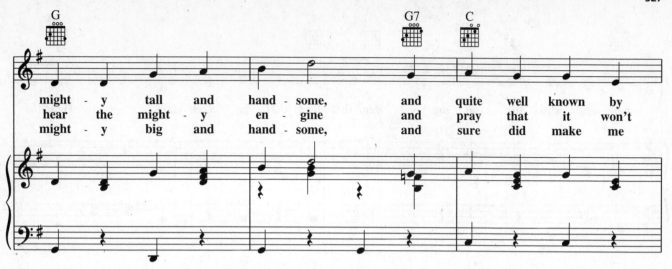

might - y   tall   and   hand - some,   and   quite   well   known   by
hear   the   might - y   en - gine   and   pray   that   it   won't
might - y   big   and   hand - some,   and   sure   did   make   me

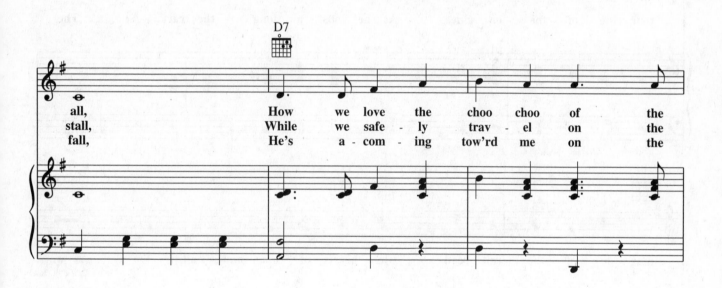

all,   How   we   love   the   choo   choo   of   the
stall,   While   we   safe - ly   trav - el   on   the
fall,   He's   a - com - ing   tow'rd   me   on   the

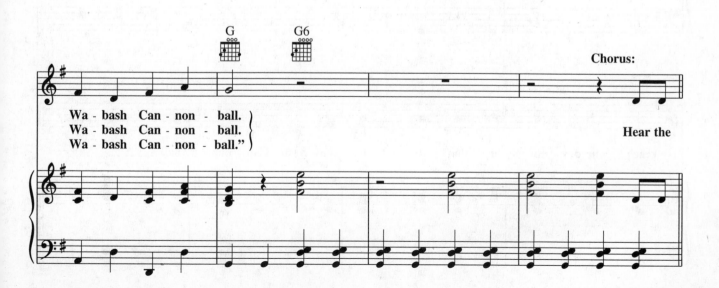

Chorus:

Wa - bash   Can - non - ball.
Wa - bash   Can - non - ball.
Wa - bash   Can - non - ball."

Hear the

bell and whis - tle call - ing, Hear the wheels that go "clack clack", Hear the

roar - ing of the en - gine, As she rolls a - long the track. The

mag - ic of the rail - road wins hearts of one and all, As we

reach our des - tin - a - tion on the Wa - bash Can - non - ball. _____

WAYFARING STRANGER

Southern American Folk Hymn

I am a poor _____ way-far-ing stran-ger, while trav'-ling
clouds _____ will ga-ther round me, I know my

through _____ this world of woe, Yet there's no sick _____ ness, toil nor
way _____ is rough and steep; But gol-den fields _____ lie out be-

dan-ger in that bright world _____ to which I go. I'm go-ing
fore me where God's re-deemed _____ shall ev-er sleep. I'm go-ing

WE GATHER TOGETHER

Words from *Nederlandtsch Gedenckclanck*
Translated by THEODORE BAKER
Netherlands Folk Melody
Arranged by EDWARD KREMSER

THE WEARING OF THE GREEN

18th Century Irish Folk Song

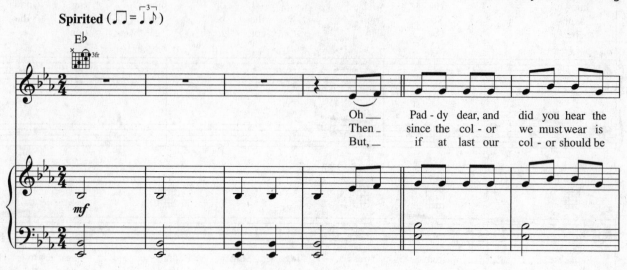

Oh __ Pad - dy dear, and did you hear the
Then, __ since the col - or we must wear is
But, __ if at last our col - or should be

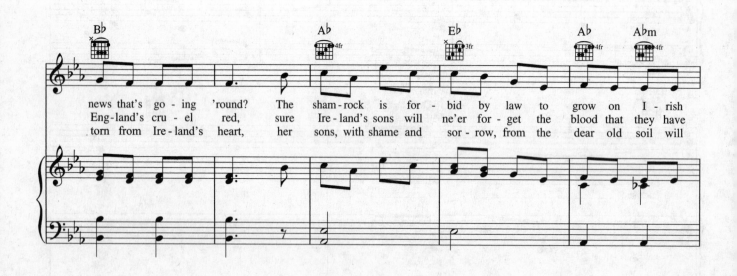

news that's go - ing 'round? The sham - rock is for - bid by law to grow on I - rish
Eng - land's cru - el red, sure Ire - land's sons will ne'er for - get the blood that they have
torn from Ire - land's heart, her sons, with shame and sor - row, from the dear old soil will

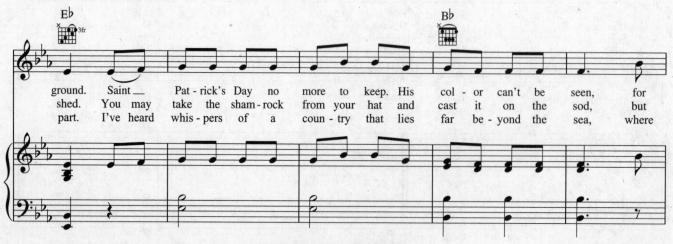

ground. Saint __ Pat - rick's Day no more to keep. His col - or can't be seen, for
shed. You may take the sham - rock from your hat and cast it on the sod, but
part. I've heard whis - pers of a coun - try that lies far be - yond the sea, where

WHEN JOHNNY COMES MARCHING HOME

Words and Music by
PATRICK SARSFIELD GILMORE

When John-ny comes march-ing

home a-gain, Hur - rah! _____ Hur - rah! _____ we'll

give him a heart - y wel - come then, Hur -

WHEN THE SAINTS GO MARCHING IN

Words by KATHERINE E. PURVIS
Music by JAMES M. BLACK

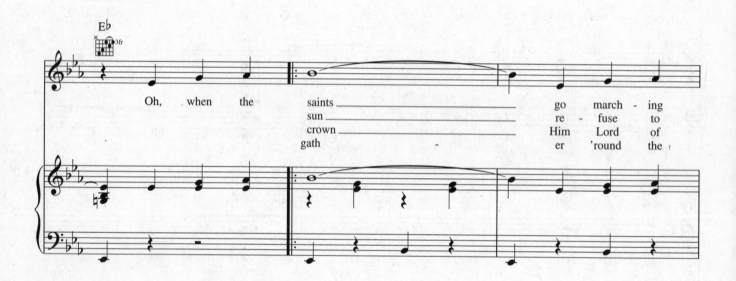

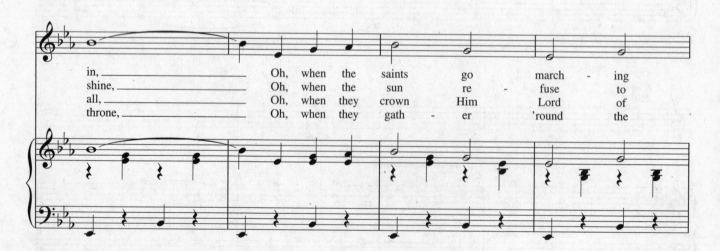

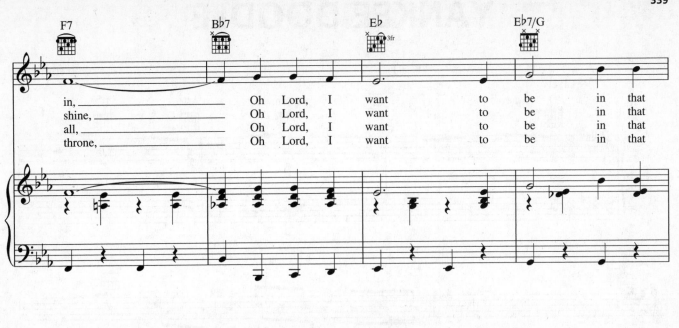

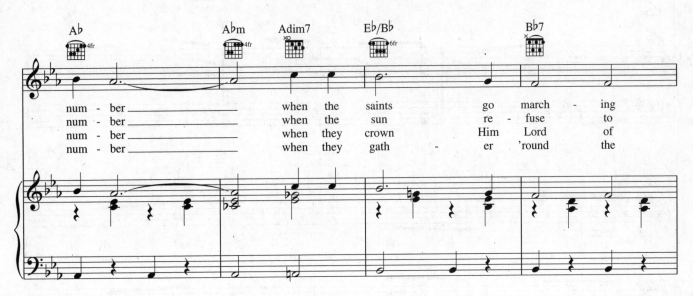

YANKEE DOODLE

Traditional

WHOOPEE TI-YI-YO, GIT ALONG

Traditional Cowboy Song

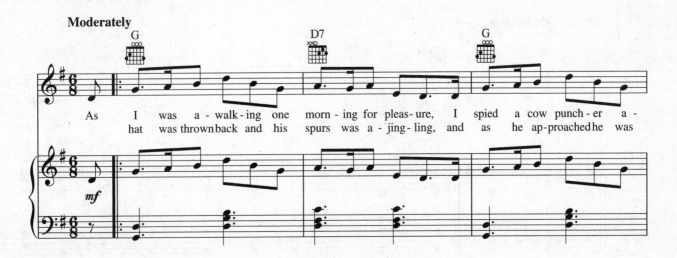

WILL THE CIRCLE BE UNBROKEN

Words by ADA R. HABERSHON
Music by CHARLES H. GABRIEL

cir - cle   be   un - bro - ken,   by   and   by,   Lord,   by   and

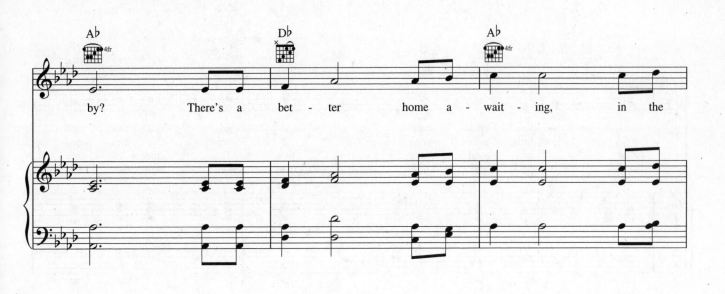

by?   There's   a   bet - ter   home   a - wait - ing,   in   the

sky,   in   the   sky.   Oh,   I   sky.
I   will

WORRIED MAN BLUES

Traditional

THE YELLOW ROSE OF TEXAS

THE YELLOW ROSE OF TEXAS

Words and Music by
J.K., 1858

0808